WHAT I WISH I ALWAYS KNEW

178
TIPS AND BITS
OF
COMMON KNOWLEDGE
AND
COMMON SENSE

LeRoy L. Carlson

To: *MARIA*

From: *LeRoy Carlson*

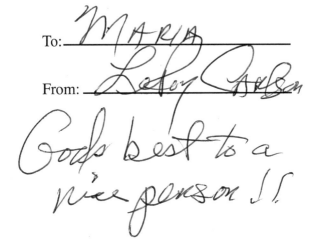

God's best to a nice person JS

Cover Design: Loren Heinzeroth

ISBN: 0-615-12906-4

To Colleen and Josh, my only wife and son.

$\mathscr{C}$ontents

$\mathcal{P}$reface

The bright rising sun in the morning signals a new day, and a new beginning for each of us. It is a gift that denotes opportunity and potential, leisure and work, helping and caring, and freedom to do and be ourselves. The new day can be a time to wonder, think, reflect or meditate. It can be as shiny and joyful as the sun, and it contains all of what we know and call *life*.

This book is about *life* and it's WHAT *I WISH I ALWAYS KNEW.* It is a book for all of us. It is for GRANDPA, GRANDMA, MOTHER, DAD, SISTER, BROTHER and FRIENDS. It is for life and living. It is common knowledge and common sense, and it's to help us live, be better persons, and enjoy life. It's to help us be our best, and do our best.

These 178 tips and bits of common knowledge and common sense are some of what I have learned and gathered along the road of life. I offer them to you with the hope that you will find them to be of interest, useful, and helpful. Some of them may be considered profound, and some are accepted etiquette. Some are what our parents taught us, tried to teach us, or now are trying to teach us. May this volume be helpful, and serve as a gentle reminder. It's *WHAT I WISH I ALWAYS KNEW.*

This book is also about saving money, which is of interest to most of us. The merchants continually tell us they will save us money in hopes that we will be inclined to make a purchase at their store. I was taught at a young age to save money, and ever since I have practiced thrift, which now complements my value system. It is my challenge and conviction.

However, I think you'd agree that we are to be good caretakers of what we possess, and should make the best use of that which we call our own. We live in a throw-away society, and it seems that when we can economize and save, we should. At the least, it behooves us to use what we have, and not be wasteful. Let us remember to conserve our natural resources; the trees, the air and more, knowing that the resources of our planet are the source of all the goods we enjoy and use.

My thanks go to new-found friends, Loren Heinzeroth from Heinzeroth Marketing Group, and Arby Arbuthnot from TAN Books and Publishers, both from Rockford Illinois, and both of whom were helpful in making this book a reality.

So, I hope you enjoy this little volume about life and living. It's *WHAT I WISH I ALWAYS KNEW.* If you benefit from it, I will be glad for you. Enjoy!

LeRoy Lind Carlson

Between You and Me

"If life had a second edition,
how I would correct the proofs."

John Clare (1793-1864)

1

Add date and identification information on everything you wish to save such as: pictures, paper clippings, documents, children's schoolwork, and appliance books. How easily we forget, even if we think we won't.

2

Learn to say *yes* and *no* with conviction. Give careful thought before taking on another assignment or task. If it's a worthy and noble cause, or will give you satisfaction, say *yes*, and do it right and well. Otherwise with a clear conscience say *no*.

3

Gently touching someone on the elbow, a pat on the back, an appropriate hug — these are simple, valuable, and profound acts. Do them often and you'll both be glad you did.

4

People express their grief in various and different ways. Some weep outwardly, and others do not, but that's who we are. When we use tears as an expression of grief, we may do so as we choose, for those tears belong to us. No two people grieve alike; so don't judge others by what you would do.

5

If you're going to remember people's birthdays, record them on a calendar at the beginning of the year. Then keep the used monthly sheets to record the birthdays on a new calendar for the next year. That's one way not to forget.

6

Include the names of the children on the tombstone(s) of the parents, and it will be much appreciated in years to come. Then there will be no doubt as to the family lineage.

7

You may enjoy reading the advice columnists in the newspapers and find them beneficial. They may have some helpful advice or a situation with which you can identify.

8

Some people read the horoscope in the newspaper, but why waste your time? Read the comics instead, for they may at least bring a laugh or smile to your face.

9

It is advantageous to memorize your Social Security number and any Personal Identification Number (PIN) you possess. As you know, they are used often — but keep them to yourself.

10

Sales are a big part of our economy, some of which necessitate personal sales calls. The hardest door for a salesperson to get through is his or her own. Therefore, determination and ambition are two good traits for a salesperson to possess.

11

Make photocopies of credit cards, driver's license, passport, and other important items from your wallet, purse, or lock box, and then store in a safe place. When traveling, carry one photocopy on your person (in a travel belt), so in case of wallet theft, needed documents can quickly be replaced.

12

Intelligence and wisdom are not the same.
Intelligence is innate, whereas wisdom comes with
experience and right decisions — it's what you do
with what you know. Keep working on that wisdom.

13

Write down that which you deem significant and important; for at any age we all have the potential to forget. In other words, don't rely on your memory.

14

We jokingly say that death and taxes are two certainties of life. The tax man comes and so does death. Plan on death and prepare for it. Be ready when the call comes, and be "right" with God and family. In that death causes separation, we grieve. To a grieving friend or relative, your help may be appreciated. Your presence may be helpful and mean more than words. When in doubt, try both.

15

$\mathbf{W}$hen you borrow something, return it when promised, and in as good or better condition than when given to you. This will help in maintaining good relationships.

16

If you loan books from your own personal library, offer a simple paper or form to be completed with the person's name and telephone number. A copy to both of you will be a reminder of ownership.

17

Time is of the essence. We all have the same amount of time each day, but no one knows how many days he will have, so use time wisely. You can control your calendar, or your calendar can control you. Be reasonable, and remember that life is short. Be aware of your time choices.

18

Be sensitive as to what you say to your kids, whether positive or negative, for they may remember it long after you're gone. You never know what they will remember.

19

My mother often said, "Procrastination is a thief of time."

So get started and do it now. Finish the task; have it over with; do not be a procrastinator. When you're done, you'll be glad you did it NOW.

20

When in doubt, get another opinion, for two heads are better than one (except maybe a cabbage head, although cabbage is good for you). After you get that second opinion, make your decision.

21

In order to leave a good legacy, create an *ethical will*, or a life story, by which you bequeath your values and a synopsis of your life to your next of kin. This *will* is not about money, but instead can include what you have learned in life: your faith and what you believe; your accomplishments and your regrets; your education, vocation, and how you earned money; family tree and family stories; tragedies, sufferings and losses; significant people and possessions in your life; and much more that you want to share with children, grandchildren, or other loved ones. Now is the time to write *your* story (or have someone write it for you) to be an accurate account of you, and you alone.

22

Laughter is good for the body, mind, and spirit. To hear a joke or funny story, to tell a joke, or read a funny story is good for us. Laughter has a way of balancing out the hardships of life. Some medical personnel even say laughter improves one's health. Others say that laughing produces fewer wrinkles than frowning.

23

Carry a metal fingernail file with you in your daily planner, pocket, or purse (but not on an airplane). You'll be surprised how many times it will get used for more than filing your nails. It's a good screwdriver, pick, poker, and more.

24

If you have a tendency to awaken at odd hours of the night, a small radio with an earplug can help pass the time, and may even lull you back to sleep. In early morning hours, you'll be surprised at the variety of radio stations picked up across the country, and the earplug will keep you from disturbing your spouse.

25

Don't forget to send a *thank you* note for a gift received or a kind deed done. It will be much appreciated and probably not soon forgotten. Also, a *phone call* will serve the same purpose, and may be cheaper than your note card and stamp. Either way, don't forget to send a thank you note, or to make the call. That's the courteous thing to do.

26

Hug your kids, your grandma, grandpa, mom, dad, and your spouse. It is good for all relationships, and will also make you feel good.

27

Go someplace or do something different to expand your horizons. Visit a museum, garden, restaurant, city, or rural area. Go to a concert, theater, church, or social event. Invite those that you do not know well over to your home. Often we get bogged down with the familiar and "safe". Try something new and different.

28

Listen to beautiful soothing music, whether it be your favorite classical, contemporary, gospel, or "oldie." It can nourish your soul, relax your mind, and calm your nerves.

A painter creates his pictures on canvas, but a musician creates on silence.

29

Know yourself. Who are you? What is your personal identity? What is your purpose in life? What are you living for? As age moves us on, we may become more reflective and introspective, and our personal history becomes more important to us. Let the activities and memories build as the days come and go. It's what we call life. For you, I hope it is good.

30

Don't major in the minors. That is, decide what's important and don't get bogged down with trivia. Life is short, so do those things that will make a difference, give satisfaction, a sense of accomplishment, and help your fellow human beings.

Body

"Every man is a builder of a temple,
called his body."

Henry David Thoreau (1817-1862)

31

Take good care of your body, keep the flab off, get proper rest and nourishment — for we have only one body, and it has to last a long time (we hope).

32

Be conscientious about using deodorant to avoid offensive body odor — often even your best friends won't mention it.

33

When you bite your fingernails, or pick your nose in public, it looks terrible, and worse than terrible. These are also things your best friends won't tell you, but your spouse might.

34

Men, be sure and shave those last whiskers under your nose, and clip the hairs that protrude from your nose and ears. This will make you look younger and more handsome, and your wife won't have to keep reminding you that those unwanted hairs should be clipped or cut.

35

As humans, we can become unhappy from the negative way in which we think about things. The mind needs to be renewed. How to do that? Visualize yourself erasing every destructive thought. Fill your mind with thoughts of God and with good and pleasant things. These happy thoughts may transform you as your mind is renewed.

36

Don't minimize memory, as it is so important. Be aware that memories are always in the making, and we want them to be pleasant and joyous. Take pictures, keep important letters and documents, and keep some of the memorabilia of your children and parents. It is true we can't always live in the past, but memory is very important, and I hope you always have yours.

37

Our bodies need rest, and so does our mind. Let the body lie down and stop acting, and let the mind stop thinking of all that needs to be done. Set aside the concerns of the day. That's rest and renewal.

38

Various aspects about us lend a positive image to others: having clean and filed nails, having no hair or dandruff left on our shoulders, carrying a clean handkerchief or tissue, and wearing polished shoes.

39

Your dentist will be happy to see you every six months, so you can retain that beautiful smile. It may be your least favorite activity, but he/she is probably a nice person. Don't forget, every six months . . . be there!

Brush and floss your teeth as your dentist tells you, but also use a little round brush that will clean between your molars next to the gums. You'll be surprised how much food collects in those areas. Give it a try, and your dentist will compliment you.

40

Get in better shape by practicing the exercise of not worrying. We may tend to worry about three things: all that's happened, all that's happening now, and all we expect to happen — yesterday, today and tomorrow. Don't attempt to bear more than one kind of trouble at once.

41

When putting on your socks, stand up — don't sit, for it's good exercise. It will cause you to seek balance and perhaps maintain more agility.

42

Before visiting your medical doctor, eye doctor, or dentist, make a list of questions you need to ask. Then be prepared to write down the answers, as exact details are later hard to recall. Ask the doctor to give a printout of any test results. Keep these to compare with your next visit. Getting a prescription? Ask the doctor what's the estimated length of usage, and what improvements or side effects might be noticed.

43

Never pick a scab on your body, for it may leave a scar and mar your beautiful body. As the aging process takes place, bumps and bruises take much longer to heal and disappear. If you're like me, you can't afford another unwanted mark on your body.

44

Men, when the elastic on your socks is too tight around your legs, simply roll down the socks one turn to release the pressure. This helps your blood circulation. Take good care of your legs; you only have two.

45

When you can't get a ring off your chubby finger, soap your hands generously, move away from the sink, or make sure the sink drain is plugged, and then carefully remove the ring. Many a ring has accidentally gone down a drain!

46

When we stand up straight, with shoulders back and head up, that good posture exudes energy and confidence . . . and it's good for our breathing.

47

Let us wash our hands often, using hot water and soap to combat the germs seeking to invade our bodies. Scrubbing hands and between fingers for ten to fifteen seconds is suggested. That's about the time it takes to sing *Happy Birthday*. When leaving a public washroom, use a paper towel to open the door, for that is one bad place for germs to congregate. It's been said, "Cleanliness is next to Godliness."

48

Nutritionists have different opinions about the amounts of fruits and vegetables, meats, dairy products, breads, etc. we should optimally consume. An easy rule of thumb may be to think about balance. If you'd really like to have just one big steak or fish for dinner, try to balance it with at least an equal amount of fruits and vegetables. If you're not hungry enough to include dairy items or bread/cereal products to balance out the meal, then plan the next meal starting with them. All major food groups contribute to a well-rounded diet, however specific choices within each food group will vary widely in potency of numerous nutrients. It's up to you to search out each food group for high-nutritional items that are right for your body.

49

Try not to lick a sharp knife, not even a steak knife, and your tongue will appreciate it. When holding an item to be chopped, curl your fingers in, which will diminish potential cuts. Use a knife by cutting away from yourself, not toward your body.

50

In a multistoried building, walk the stairs, when reasonable, instead of riding the elevator. It's good exercise. Do it often, and the result may be a stronger heart and slender body.

Cars and Trucks

"The trouble with hobby cars is,
there's just never enough space
for them in your garage."

Anonymous

51

When it's time to buy a different car or truck, don't take the old one to an auto dealership for trade. Instead, shine up the old vehicle; check a computer for the going price in the *Kelly Blue Book;* put an ad in the local newspaper or on the Internet; and sell it. Then buy a car from the paper or Internet, preferably through a private party. This procedure may take a bit longer, but you'll be surprised at how much money can be saved.

52

When *buying* a used car or truck, ask the seller questions such as: What is the mileage? Has it been in any accidents? What doesn't work on the car? What else doesn't work? Ask questions until you are satisfied that you know the vehicle's good and bad points. Copy the Vehicle Identification Number (VIN) from the car, and on the Internet you will be able to find more information. When inspecting the vehicle, check if it has been repainted, and notice carefully how the hood, headlights, and trunk fit. These are good indicators as to any accidents and bodywork done on the vehicle. When it comes time to negotiate the price, remind the seller of any items needing repair or replacement, then make your offer. Counter offers are always in order.

53

*W*hen you are in the process of *selling* your car or truck, set your price high enough, because you can always come down, but you cannot go up. When an offer is received, accept it; or if it is too low, don't be afraid to counter it, or think it over, or say "no" in a firm voice so the buyer will know your intention. Also, don't be afraid if two "lookers" come at the same time, for it will be to your advantage, as it will create competition.

54

A leased car or truck may have the advantage of no large initial capital expenditure, but may cost more in the long run, because one does not own the vehicle at the end of the lease. Yet for some people, leasing may be a desirable arrangement. If your vehicle is part of a business, you can advantageously deduct the cost of the lease on your taxes as a business expense. Run the numbers both ways.

55

Even though stipulated in the owner's manual or on the dashboard, it may not be necessary to use premium gasoline in your automobile. Chances are very good it will perform the same on the less expensive regular grade. Give it a try, and notice the money you will save.

56

Here are a variety of ways to increase gas mileage:
Empty the trunk! Sporting goods, tools, and overdue library books can all weigh down your car unnecessarily.

Avoid jack-rabbit starts.

Avoid excessive warm-up time. Modern engines do not require it.

Don't leave the engine idling while waiting for a long period of time.

Keep your speed at 55 miles per hour or less whenever possible.

Try to keep your speed constant. Use cruise control when on long stretches of flat road.

57

Consider buying a car or truck that is one to five years old, for it is probably "just like new," nicely broken in, and has already depreciated some or much. This way the cost and/or monthly payment will be considerably less, and if you choose, you may be able to afford a more luxurious model.

58

Purchased windshield washer fluid is necessary in the winter because it doesn't freeze. But in warmer months you can use plain water. It will have the same effect as rainwater — to keep those windshields clean.

59

Keep your engine and hoses clean. The hoses will last longer, they will all look better, and at sale time it will show your care of the car.

60

If or when you borrow someone's car or truck, return it with the gas tank full. It's a fair exchange and a kind gesture, and you'll be remembered for your generosity.

61

Always carry battery jumper cables and a first aid kit in your car or truck, for these are common items needed in emergency situations.

62

Thieves can see the Vehicle Identification Number (VIN) of your car through the front left windshield. They can then take the number to a dealer, have a set of keys made, and steal your car. Therefore, place a piece of dark tape over the number, or at least a part of it. It's illegal to remove the number, but you can cover it up. Your car also has its VIN number in other various places on the body, but not visible to the "bad guys".

63

If you're concerned about dents in the side of your car or truck, be careful where you park, especially in a striped parking lot. Try not to park too close to an adjacent vehicle. An end-of-the-lot parking space is often the most desirable, and will often avoid that unwanted dent or ding.

64

Don't forget that periodic oil change, and also check the air pressure in your tires once each month — certainly before a long road trip. Proper tire pressure will prolong the life of your tires, and may even save a bit of gas.

65

If repair work is needed on your car or truck, you may want to find a person who does work in his own garage, or consider a small repair shop in your city. These places will probably be cheaper than the large car dealer, unless your warranty is in effect. Your repair job is as good or bad as the person doing it.

haracter

"Great persons are able to do great kindnesses."

Miguel De Cervantes (1547-1616)

66

If we've had a standing disagreement with someone, we'd do well to swallow our pride and reconcile, for it's later than we think. It's always appropriate to make things right with the other person. We will probably then sleep better.

67

When you are wrong, say so . . . admit it, and don't try to rationalize an error or mistake. Until you are able to take responsibility for your decisions and action, you will be looking for a scapegoat to blame for your problems. Our admission of wrong says a great deal about our character.

68

Unfortunately greed is a part of our nature, especially as it pertains to money and things. We never have enough. Epicurus, the Greek philosopher said, "If you wish to make a man happy, add not to his possessions, but take away from his desires. To whom little is not enough, nothing is enough." In terms of money it seems that "enough" is never achievable. Greed prevails.

69

A kind deed to someone will most often change our mood and raise our spirits. Give it a try.

70

Dad may love us dearly, yet often will not know how to show it.

71

Whatever our parents have taught us, and all that we've learned in life; we will do well to remember that there is still much more to learn . . . very much more.

72

The better we know a person, the more faults and foibles we will discover. But don't be disappointed, because it works both ways. Chalk it all up to being human, and look for the best in each other.

73

Remember that life is full of second chances, but the initial *right decision* is the better.

74

We can tell a lot about a person by the way he reacts when receiving a traffic ticket, or losing his luggage at the airport.

75

A smile goes a long way, so be intentional and smile often, especially when you see or meet someone you don't know. It eases fear, and causes comfort. Give it a try.

76

No one is perfect; not even you or me, our grandmother, Sunday School teacher, favorite aunt, uncle, or author.

77

Assuming the service is good, tip the waitress and waiter in a generous manner, for that is their livelihood. It will make them and you feel good, for generosity causes good feelings.

78

Never refuse a gift. There is joy in giving, and for someone to give, there must be a recipient. To refuse a gift is a disappointment to the giver. If we find the gift received not useable, give it away, then we too will have the joy of giving.

79

Sometimes we have the right to be angry, especially when someone else has been wronged; but that never gives us the right to be unkind or cruel.

80

Attitude is vitally important! The difference between winners and losers in athletic contests often is that winners see themselves as winning and losers give themselves an excuse to lose. Experiments indicate if a teacher thinks she has a gifted class, she visualizes and treats the students as such, and they perform as gifted. It's a self-fulfilling prophecy familiar to salespersons, educators, and all of us.

81

A good leader is driven by an invigorating will to succeed. He/she has vision that captures eager followers. A good leader must have competence and confidence, but also graciousness and humility. He's a *team member* who leads the team to the right answer.

82

Let us be kind to our parents, enjoy them now, remembering all their care and benefits to us. We will undoubtedly miss them after they are deceased. Now is the time.

83

If someone says something unkind about you, live your life so others will not believe it.

84

When a seemingly poor person, maybe on the street, asks for money, let us give what we are able and what our conscience dictates. We may never know if the person has an honest need, but we do have money in *our* pocket, so it's better to err on the side of generosity.

85

When walking across the street in front of a car at a stop sign, walk with haste to let the driver know you are aware he is waiting to drive on. It's a small courteous gesture, and so much nicer than trying to take all the time you can to cross the street.

86

Forgiveness is always appropriate and good. Let us be the first to ask for forgiveness, even when we have not been asked. Let us forgive, even when the other person doesn't know she has hurt us. If we find forgiving difficult to do, that means we are human. Let's strive to do it anyway. It takes a change of heart. Not forgiving may fester anger and bitterness; but to forgive can bring release, contentment, satisfaction, and a sense of accomplishment.

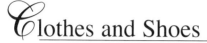Clothes and Shoes

"**Probably every new and eagerly expected garment ever put on since clothes came in, fell a trifle short of the wearer's expectation.**"

Charles Dickens (1812-1870)

87

When shining our shoes, a rag will work well, but try using a shoe brush. It gives a good shine, plus gets into all the cracks and crevices of the shoes.

88

When putting on shoes, consider using a shoehorn. The backs of your shoes won't break down as quickly, so they'll look nice longer. Use a long-handled shoehorn and eliminate bending over.

89

Instead of joining this throwaway society, learn to patch your socks! Simply purchase iron-on patches from a dollar store or fabric center. The result is twice as much wear.

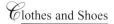

90

A man's freshly starched shirt is very smooth and dressy (even if it may be less comfortable to wear). Ironing a shirt isn't too hard, and it does save money. After spraying starch on the cuffs and collar — press the cuffs and sleeves first, then the back, the two fronts, and the collar last. Since wrinkles on the collar top are quite noticeable, quickly press the underside, but precisely press the top to be wrinkle free.

91

When one sock wears out, recycle it as a rag. However, you may want to keep the good one to wear with another sock of similar color or style. Probably no one will know the difference if worn at night. To be even more frugal: When you find a particular sock you really like, buy several identical pairs. They'll be easy to match when they come out of the dryer!

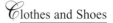

92

One may want to use that new or fine piece of clothing or perfume right now, and as often as you like. What are you saving it for? Enjoy it now! (This goes for fine china and family antiques also.)

93

Women, more than men, have been into "having their colors analyzed" to determine what colors and tones look best with their complexion and coloring. Men could also benefit knowing what color values make them look alive and vibrant, or tired and drab. Two good sources of information are your wife and a female sales person at a quality-clothing store. They'll spend time with you to see if the bright colors in the jungle patterned shirt look better next to your skin than the muted colors in the pastel shirt.

94

Men, carry your wallet in alternate back trouser pockets, in alternate years, and notice that it will prevent or prolong holes from wearing in the trouser pocket area. Today's wallet is big with many credit cards and papers.

95

To keep clothes smelling good in dresser drawers, clip the perfumed tabs from magazine and newspaper inserts. Tuck them among clothes in the drawers and soon you'll notice a pleasant aroma.

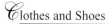

96

When needing to purchase an item, consider other sources before visiting the department store or big box store. EBay, second-hand stores, garage sales, and estate sales are valuable places to save money on most any item. Remember not all things have to be purchased new to serve your purpose.

97

Buy shoes in the late afternoon, because at that time of day your feet tend to swell a bit. Therefore, you will acquire a more comfortable fit.

98

Men, you'll look neater if you keep your necktie knot tight at the top of your shirt. That is, don't let the top of your shirt show above the tie. Keep it tight.

Conversation

"We reproach people for talking about themselves; but it is the subject they treat best."

Anatole France (1844-1924)

99

When making a personal introduction of one person to another, help each hear and remember names by talking slowly and with direct eye contact. Repeating names twice will be appreciated.

100

Conversation is an important art, yet often not practiced well. It's been said that the trouble with a gal who talks too much, is that she's liable to say something she has not thought of yet. We tend to like hearing ourselves talk and to tell each other more than we know. But, good conversation includes both talking and listening. Take time to really hear another's ideas, convictions and perspective. Learn to disagree without being disagreeable. In the end, you may learn that the less you say, the more people will remember.

101

In a telephone conversation, the one who initiates the call, most often has the prerogative to terminate it.

102

We are so accustomed to our own telephone number that we often "rattle it off" with great speed at the end of a voice mail. Say the number *slowly* and speak the last few digits as clearly as the beginning ones, not letting your voice trail off. The recipient of your voice mail may have never heard your number before and has just one chance to write it down.

103

In a social gathering, you may see two or three people talking and wish to join in the conversation. It's tempting to step right up and start talking. However, do realize that your presence or greeting is no more important than those already talking together. Stand close by, but don't speak until someone in the group recognizes you and chooses to include you in the conversation. They may be having a private conversation and then you should return later.

104

Even in a small gathering, people may not know or remember each other's names. Be sensitive to this fact and be willing to take the initiative in introducing people. When you'd like to introduce someone to a group, but are afraid you won't remember all the names, just say, "I'm not sure you all know 'Mary' so why don't we go around the circle and tell her our names."

105

Some people may think profanity is cool. But to others, use of profanity will surely diminish your character, reputation, and image. Is it worth that?

106

Never take God's name in vain, for it is definitely contrary to the Ten Commandments of the Bible.

107

When we speak an untruth, it will most likely require another one. Let us be honest, so we won't have to take the time to think of another explanation or excuse.

108

A telephone call, note, or card to a friend or loved one is money very well spent. We don't need to have a reason. All we need is to *care* enough to send a greeting or say hello, and to remember people often.

109

In deciding to express kindness, you will always find it to be the right decision.

110

Make an intentional effort to affirm people. Large or small compliments about job achievements, weight, clothes, children, disposition, or whatever, are good places to start. But make sure your compliments are *sincere* and show true appreciation. Don't compliment others just to make a good impression. Everyone has the need to be valued, so find the good qualities and express them.

111

Let us say kind words about people long before their funeral, and we'll probably never regret it.

112

If we want a secret or confidence to remain as such, *never* share it — not even with the "fence post" or with our best friend.

113

When parting company, especially family, do so with kind words, for we never know when it will be the last word.

114

When visiting with someone, watch his body language. Fidgeting and looking elsewhere may tell you he's ready to conclude the conversation.

115

Joking and kidding are fun with friends and acquaintances, but don't use the occasion to vent negative jabs or zings.

116

If we want to be good conversationalists, let us ask questions, listen, use good eye contact, and show interest in the other person(s). Our turn will come to talk, but let us talk only sparingly about ourselves, unless asked.

117

When someone extends a greeting with the words "How are you?" or "How's it going?" we may do well to receive it as a greeting and not as a literal question. Perhaps a better greeting is "Good morning" or "Hello."

We also are quick to respond by saying, "Fine," whether we mean it or not. If you really want to know how someone is, ask a more specific question.

118

It is prudent to have a dictionary, large or small, next to our easy chair, to look up new words found in our reading. If you choose, jot down the words and definitions in a handy notebook, and refer to it periodically and add these new words to your vocabulary.

# Home

"There is no place more delightful
than home."

Marcus Tullius Cicero (106-43 B.C.)

119

Buy the paper towel roll with the smaller perforated sheets. Often one does not need a large sheet to complete a task, and this type of roll will last longer. Hang a roll of towels in the garage, as well as in the utility room and basement. You'll be prepared for all sorts of dilemmas.

120

Hang a decorative set of bells on the inside of your home entrance door. You will hear the "jingle" when someone enters or exits and be alerted to their presence.

121

For two people in the home, don't put the dirty dishes in the dishwasher after each small meal. Simply take them to the sink, wash quickly under the faucet with hot sudsy water, then place them right back on the table where they'll be ready for the next meal. Overall, it's a time saver.

122

Refrain from buying a pen or pencil; free ones can be found at service companies, conventions or fairs. Calendars and small paper pads may also be found at these places.

123

Each person living in a home deserves to have some area, be it large or small, which is hers alone. Even when sharing a bedroom, a child can have a chair, bookshelf, or drawer to herself.

124

Choose two dates in the year to do a home safety check — maybe January 1 and June 1, or the first day of spring and fall. Check any smoke alarm batteries, change your furnace filter, and add new carbon monoxide detector batteries. Examine the main water valve coming into the house, as well as those under the toilets. Giving them a maintenance twist (off and on) will help prevent sticking in the future. Check the water heater manual for information about draining sediment from the bottom of the tank. Repeat fire exit instructions to your family.

125

When a three-way light bulb has burned out, chances are good that one of the lower wattage settings still works. Test the bulb to verify if true, then label and store until it's subsequently needed in a socket requiring the lower wattage setting.

126

If you feel you need a security system in your home, by all means have one. However, if you think you can't afford an electrical system, your family can still ward off intruders. Purchase security company decals from a locksmith or hardware store and place in several windows and doors. Add a "beware of dog" sign on your gate, or place a huge dog bowl by the back door to make an intruder think twice about entering your premises.

Money

"Put not your trust in money,
but put your money in trust."

Oliver Wendell Holmes (1809-1894)

127

We must not let money consume or control us, for it has the power and ability to do just that. We may never feel that we have enough money, no matter how much we have. The very wealthy man was asked how much money he needed, and he answered, "just a little more." Let us keep it all in perspective, be thankful, and enjoy what we do have.

128

Make a strong effort to pay your credit card bill in full each month, otherwise there can be a high interest rate or late fee on the unpaid balance. If you are carrying large unpaid balances on several cards, first start paying off the card with the highest annual percentage rate. Be careful about closing an account, for that may negatively affect your credit score. If helpful, cut up the cards, or put them in some exotic place, such as your food freezer, to remain out of reach.

129

Be sure to take advantage of your employer's pension or payroll savings plan. Contribute as much as you can, especially if your employer will match your contribution. Some day you'll be glad you did.

130

Some people like to possess a second credit card with a very low credit limit. This card is used for Internet or phone purchases. Therefore, a thief cannot charge much on this account, and your first card is still useable for immediate needs.

131

Buy generic drugs when possible. Ask both your doctor and pharmacist for comparable brand and generic names, and I think you'll be surprised by the money you can save.

132

Ask your doctor if he/she happens to have some samples of your prescription drug. Often that is the case and you might be the recipient of his/her added generosity. The pharmaceutical companies are quite generous, and someone has to use the sample drugs. It might as well be you.

133

If or when you get a raise or bonus at work, try to save at least one half of it, for it's a very painless way to save.

134

If you are thinking of buying a *big* boat, and you must ask the price, then you can't afford it.

135

Don't make impulsive purchases, especially on large items. Wait a day or two, and then if the item still seems important to you, buy it. The three-day "cooling off" law in most states is for impulsive buyers.

136

To control money, one must know how much he has and where it is being spent. Saving purchase receipts, keeping a record book, and planning a categorized budget are useful tools to develop control. Be sure to include budget lines for savings and long-term goals. Some people place money for each monthly budgeted item in separate envelopes to limit overspending.

137

A credit card that gives air miles, even though you may pay a fee, will often be advantageous. However, figure the cost of the card — if you are using it enough to get an adequate number of miles, and if it is worth the free travel received. It may be a good value, but do the math and know for sure.

138

Don't always skimp and save so much money for the distant future that you can't enjoy the present. Plan to allow money for small family events, as well as a big trip in the future. Go for it and create lots of memories!

139

The most economical way to purchase a large item, such as an automobile or boat, is to plan well ahead, and *borrow money from yourself.* This is accomplished by *making payments to yourself* by putting money in your bank for a 3-5 year period. After you have saved and banked money for that period of time, use it to purchase your item. In this manner you avoid *paying interest* on a loan for the purchased item, and instead *get interest* from the bank for your saved money. And you will now own your new item free and clear.

140

Save as much money as your budget will allow, and don't spend money just for the sake of spending. Buy only what you need. And don't spend money just to irritate or anger your spouse, for it's very immature, and injurious to the marital relationship.

141

If possible, try hard to keep an *emergency account* of some kind to cover any basic emergency needs that may arise in your family. The amount should preferably cover at least a three-month period of time.

142

You will do well to only use your own bank's ATM machine, for then you will avoid a maintenance fee. Those *small* fees will add up faster than you think.

143

Money *saved* (preferably consistently, like weekly or monthly), plus interest *earned*, plus *time*, equals a large sum of money for retirement or a "rainy day". Time, time, time is of the essence. Put your money in the bank, or in stocks or bonds. You may want to use a product that is tax sheltered. One method of saving is to use an Individual Retirement Account (IRA), either a traditional or Roth. For example, if you can save $4000 per year at a 6.5% annual rate of return, in 40 years you will have about $780,000. That's what time does, and that's a lot of money. Ask your banker or financial planner.

144

Term insurance, with its own purpose, is most often adequate, and probably a better value than whole life insurance, which may pay interest, but usually at a much lower interest rate than your local bank. Check it out.

145

To protect your identity, shred papers which include your personal pertinent information and numbers. You will find the cost of a shredder to be well worth it.

146

Don't print or write your Social Security number or driver's license number on your bank checks. Those numbers must be kept confidential.

147

Do not carry a Social Security card in your purse or wallet, lest it get lost or stolen. With a Social Security number, a thief can obtain much personal information to steal your identity, then perhaps your bank accounts, credit cards, home, etc.

148

Check your credit rating every year with one or more of the major credit bureaus. In doing so, you'll know if there is any incorrect or injurious information. If so, deal with it immediately.

149

Barter or trade goods and services, and you may be happy with substantial savings. Be aware that some transactions may have tax consequences. Check with your accountant.

150

If possible, buy your own home, and when mortgage rates decline, refinance or modify your loan. Modifying a loan is a simpler process than refinancing, and usually done by your bank, rather than a mortgage company. You'll be pleasantly surprised by the new loan's lower monthly payment, the shorter completion time of the loan, and the total lesser amount paid for your home.

Additional mortgage tips: Make an extra mortgage payment when you can, which will be applied directly to the principal of the loan. Or set your mortgage payments to be paid every two weeks. Both will result in significant interest savings. These are big items, so don't miss them.

151

Remember that many items you purchase, sooner or later need repair and maintenance, which can be time-consuming and costly. Consider that possibility before making your purchase. If you don't need the item, don't buy it.

152

In estate planning, parents mean well in trying to treat their kids equally. To be equal, take into account any education bills you have paid, money given for special projects, loans, etc. Remember, even though you may not be keeping a scorecard, the kids probably are.

153

Buy printed checks from one of the many companies found in magazine and paper advertisements. You will probably find them to be less expensive than what your bank offers.

154

When buying homeowner's insurance, remember that you need not insure your home for its total value. The land, perhaps 10-30% of your home value, is indestructible and need not be insured. Ask your insurance agent.

155

To save money on your homeowner's insurance, request a *higher deductible amount* on your policy. The deductible is the amount *you* will pay on the claim before the insurance company pays. Of course, a higher deductible means you must be prepared to pay a larger initial amount for any filed claim. An additional advantage of a higher deductible policy is that you'll be less apt to file a small claim, keeping the insurance company from possibly raising your rates or canceling the insurance. Ask your agent.

156

It's fun to support and attend your city's professional orchestra, theater, and fine arts programs, but also remember that the local high school, college, and university offer many *free* or inexpensive programs. Save money by enjoying free festivals and concerts in the park.

157

Don't forget to make a *will*, and then periodically update it. If you die without a will, the state will make one for you, where your assets may not be distributed as you'd like. Depending on your family situation, you may want to establish a *trust* to offer tax and other advantages to your next of kin. For each account within the trust, know its location and content. Be sure it bears the trust name. Discuss financial plans with your family, financial planner, attorney, or trust company.

158

In legal documents, such as wills, trusts, insurance policies, stocks and bonds, when referring to your children, list their specific names and not use only the words, "the children." Check details with your attorney.

159

If you are a *senior citizen,* don't forget the Early Bird Specials and the Senior Menu offered by local restaurants. Some may have a 10% discount to senior citizens. These are kind gestures on the part of the merchants, but don't be presumptuous — a hearty thank you is always in order. Tell your friends so they too can patronize these good places.

# Religion

"It was a common saying among the
Puritans, 'Brown bread and
the Gospel is good fare.' "

Matthew Henry (1662-1714)

160

In Matthew's Gospel in the Bible, Jesus says, "So in everything, do to others what you would have them do to you . . ."

This is the Golden Rule of the Christian faith, and Jesus stated it in a positive way.

161

Jesus said in Mark's Gospel, "Love the Lord your God with all your heart and with all your soul and with all your mind and with all your strength."
". . . Love your neighbor as yourself. There's no commandment greater than these."

The first quotation is known as the *Shema.* Jesus, in his Jewish tradition, along with other pious Jews, most likely recited this twice a day. The second quote, Jesus added to show that love for neighbor is a natural and logical outgrowth of love for God.

162

St. Augustine in the fourth century said that we are to "love God and do what we please."

When we love God *first*, and then do what we please, it will be the right thing, and it will then please God and us too.

163

"Who is wise and understanding among you? Let him show it by his good life, by deeds done in the humility that comes from wisdom." "But the wisdom that comes from heaven is first of all pure; then peace-loving, considerate, submissive, full of mercy and good fruit, impartial and sincere." This is from the writer James, in the Bible.

164

The Bible in Second Timothy says, "For God did not give us a spirit of timidity, but a spirit of power, of love and of self-discipline."

There's a force more powerful than fear or timidity, and that is love. Through dependence on God, we gain confidence and self-control. Practice this, and fear and timidity will diminish.

165

The Bible in Paul's epistle to the Romans says, "If you confess with your mouth, 'Jesus is Lord,' and believe in your heart that God raised him from the dead, you will be saved."

"In your heart" means that we believe in Jesus not only with our emotions and affections, but also with our intellect and will. "Raised from the dead" means that Christians believe not only that Jesus lived, but also that He still lives today.

166

From the Psalms, in the Bible:
"Hear my prayer, O Lord; listen to my cry for mercy. In the day of my trouble I will call to you, for you will answer me."

Quiet times are the key to a close personal relationship with God. Prayer is one of the most important keys to good quiet times.

167

In the Bible, in John's Gospel, Jesus says, "I am the way, and the truth, and the life. No one comes to the Father except through me."

Jesus is the one way road to God.

168

The Bible in Paul's epistle to the churches of Galatia says, ". . . the fruit of the Spirit is love, joy, peace, patience, kindness, goodness, faithfulness, gentleness and self-control."

These are virtues of the Christian faith and Christian characteristics that are produced by the Holy Spirit.

169

In the Bible, in John's Gospel, Jesus says, "For God so loved the world that he gave his one and only Son, that whoever believes in him shall not perish but have eternal life."

ravel

"I always like to begin a journey on
Sundays, because I shall have the prayers
of the church to preserve
all that travel by land or by water."

Jonathan Swift (1667-1745)

170

The first-class section of the airplane is preferable and more comfortable, but all sections of the airplane will arrive at the destination at the same time.

171

The most spacious seats in the coach section of the aircraft are in the exit rows or galley rows. However, the galley rows have no seats in front of them, therefore belongings cannot be stored underneath.

172

Be aware of the hour for picking up your rental car. A same or similar return time of day may save you an extra hourly charge, or even a full day charge.

173

When staying in a motel/hotel, use only the towels etc. that you need. Also, don't upset the room more than necessary. It's a common courtesy, and the maid will appreciate it.

174

If your budget will allow it, take at least one international trip each year, as it will more rapidly expand your world perspective and view.

175

Check out the "low cost" airlines for your next flight. For that lower cost, you may not get an "assigned" seat, but that may be the only difference. Everything else is probably the same. The worst that can happen is that with a random seat, you may sit in the back of the aircraft, or in a center seat. But for a one or two hour flight, your body can probably endure any seat, and that "low cost" will put a smile on your face, and money in your pocket.

176

The best value on redeemed air miles is an overseas trip, or flights that are valued at over $300. For instance, a free $125 flight is not a good value. Do the math and figure it out.

177

If you have an abundant amount of air miles that you may never be able to use, inquire as to whether they can be used by another person. You may want to give them to someone instead of letting them go to waste. Be realistic, will you ever be able to use all of them?

178

When you are a guest in a home, a three day stay may be the limit, unless you are sure, sure, sure that a longer stay will be appreciated by your host and hostess. You've probably heard it said that a stay longer than three days is like a dead fish; after three days there's an odor.